Brown v. Board of Education

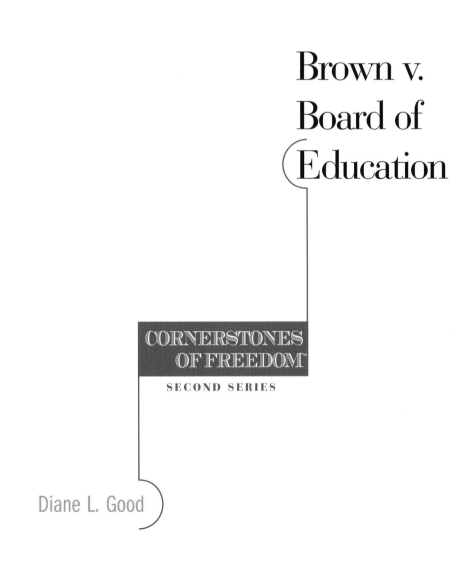

CORNERSTONES
OF FREEDOM™

SECOND SERIES

Diane L. Good

Children's Press®
A Division of Scholastic Inc.
New York • Toronto • London • Auckland • Sydney
Mexico City • New Delhi • Hong Kong
Danbury, Connecticut

Photographs © 2004: AP/Wide World Photos: 27 (Lou Krasky), cover top, 21, 23, 32, 37, 38; Brown Brothers: 7, 9, 11, 12; Corbis Images: 6, 19, 29, 30, 31, 34, 35, 36, 39, 44 center, 44 right, 45 top right (Bettmann), 15; Getty Images: 10 (Hulton Archive), 25 (National Archive/Newsmakers); Hulton|Archive/Getty Images: 13, 14, 20, 40, 45 bottom; Index Stock Imagery/Ewing Galloway: 26; National Archives and Records Administration: 3, 5, 24 (Mid Atlantic Region, Philadelphia), 22, 28 (Southeast Region, Atlanta); Photri Inc.: cover bottom, 18, 33, 44 left; Superstock, Inc.: 8, 17; The Image Works: 16, 45 top left (Joe Sohm), 41 (Topham).

Library of Congress Cataloging-in-Publication Data
Good, Diane L.
   Brown v. Board of Education: a civil rights milestone / Diane L. Good.
      p. cm. — (Cornerstones of freedom. Second series)
   Explains the history of segregation in the United States and cases that tested the law allowing "separate but equal" treatment, including the five cases that came together as Brown v. Board of Education.
   Includes bibliographical references (p.) and index.
      ISBN 0-516-24225-3
      1.Brown, Oliver, 1918—Trials, litigation, etc.—Juvenile literature.
2. Topeka (Kan.). Board of Education—Trials, litigation, etc.—Juvenile literature. 3. Segregation in education—Law and legislation—United States—Juvenile literature. 4. African Americans—Civil rights—Juvenile literature. [1. Brown, Oliver, 1918—Trials, litigation, etc. 2. Segregation in education—Law and legislation. 3. African Americans—Civil rights.] I. Title. II. Series.
KF228.B76G66 2004
344.73'0798—dc21

                                            2003009097

1 2 3 4 5 6 7 8 9 10 R 13 12 11 10 09 08 07 06 05 04

BARBARA JOHNS STRAIGHTENED her collar as she looked in the mirror. She was a bit afraid, but she was determined. Barbara, Carrie Stokes, and a small group of friends at Robert Moton High School in Farmville, Virginia, were taking action. They were tired of going to classes in overcrowded "tar-paper shacks." They wanted a better school and newer books. They wanted an auditorium with real seats, not just folding chairs. They wanted the same education white students got in Farmville.

★ ★ ★ ★

Barbara's school was **segregated**. For the past six months, Barbara and her friends held secret meetings to work out the details of their plan. By April 23, 1951, they were ready. That day at school, one of the boys made a telephone call to Principal Boyd Jones. He told Jones that some students were in trouble downtown, prompting the principal to leave the building. When Jones was safely gone, the friends sent notes to the teachers that said all students were to report to the auditorium for an assembly. The notes were signed "B.J."—Principal Boyd Jones (or Barbara Johns).

In the auditorium, Barbara and Carrie moved quickly to the stage. They made a moving speech, telling the students of their plan to go on strike to demand better schools. Barbara and Carrie explained that they had already talked to members of the school board, who had ignored their concerns. Perhaps the publicity a strike would attract would bring about change. Students would come to school each day, but they would not attend classes until changes were made.

Barbara and Carrie had no idea they would become part of a lawsuit that would go all the way to the U.S. Supreme Court. They did not want their school to be **integrated**; they just wanted their school for African American students to be equal to the school for white students in Farmville. While Barbara and Carrie were planning their strike, parents in other communities across the country were also working to improve their local schools. This movement would result in a landmark Supreme Court case known as *Brown et al. v. Board of Education of Topeka et al.*

SEGREGATION

We tend to classify ourselves as "us" and "them." When we meet someone new, we want to know if that person is more like us or more different from us. These differences can sometimes be scary. Segregation laws were passed in the United States to keep "us" away from "them."

Farmville, Virginia, was a segregated community southwest of Richmond. This photo of the white school compared to that of the African-American school (shown on page 3) clearly shows that the two schools were anything but equal.

KEEPING PEOPLE APART

Today, students of all colors across the United States learn, play, and grow together, but it has not always been that way. For many years, public schools in some states were segregated, so African American children would not go to the same schools as white children did. In 1954, the United

This photo of a segregated classroom in the 1940s was typical of many African-American schools at that time. Classrooms were overcrowded and often in poor condition.

States Supreme Court ruled in *Brown v. Board of Education* that segregation in schools was **unconstitutional**. This ruling put an end to legal segregation. The story of *Brown v. Board of Education* spanned nearly one hundred years and involved hundreds of people across the United States.

LIFE BEFORE BROWN V. BOARD OF EDUCATION

Slavery existed in parts of the United States for nearly two hundred years before the Civil War ended in 1865. Even when African Americans were no longer **enslaved**, they were not considered citizens. White citizens could vote, but African Americans could not. Even African Americans who were free before the Civil War had never been citizens.

In 1866, Congress passed the Fourteenth Amendment to the Constitution, and all people born in the United States became citizens. Every citizen is entitled to certain **civil rights** that are spelled out in the Bill of Rights, which is made up of the first ten constitutional amendments. The Fourteenth Amendment says that individual states cannot make laws to take away a person's right to life, liberty, or property.

This illustration shows a slave trade auction in the 1850s. African-American slaves were treated as property to be bought and sold among white landowners.

★ ★ ★ ★

Still, many white people found it difficult to accept African Americans as equals. Many white people thought that former slaves should not own land, vote, or attend public schools. African Americans could say little about how they lived because they were often kept from voting. For example, some states passed laws that required people own property or be able to read in order to vote, and most African Americans could not meet these requirements.

Even after the Civil War, many African Americans lived in the shadow of slavery. This photograph shows free black women in South Carolina in 1899.

★ ★ ★ ★

Comfortable, well-kept classrooms such as this one in Evanston, Illinois, were typical of many white schools.

Segregation laws made it legal to keep African Americans separate from whites as long as both groups had access to equal facilities. This idea was known as **"separate but equal."** Facilities for African Americans, however, were rarely equal to those for whites. Schools for white children had comfortable desks in the classrooms, central heating, and flush toilets. Schools for African American children had unheated classrooms with benches for desks and outdoor toilets.

TESTING THE LAWS

Even before they were citizens, some African American parents began asking the courts to overrule the segregation laws. In 1849, five-year-old Sarah Roberts walked past five Boston elementary schools for white children on her way to the segregated school she attended. Her father asked the members of the school board to reassign her to a closer school, but they refused. Sarah's father, Benjamin, filed a lawsuit against the City of Boston. The Massachusetts Supreme Court ruled that Boston had the right to have segregated schools, and Benjamin Roberts lost his case. However, in 1855, Massachusetts passed a law to end segregation in public schools.

In 1896, another lawsuit was filed that challenged segregation. In Louisiana, people traveled by railroad in segregated railcars—whites sat in the front cars and African Americans sat in the back cars. Homer Plessy was an African American who boarded the train in one of the front cars. The conductor told him to move to the back of the train, but Plessy refused and was arrested. In court, Plessy argued that the railroad companies did not have the right to segregate their cars because segregation was a violation of his Fourteenth Amendment rights. Plessy's case went to the U.S. Supreme Court, which ruled that segregation was legal as long as the accommodations given to both groups were equal. It would be more than fifty years before segregation would be declared illegal.

BRIDGING DIFFERENCES

Around 1915, many African Americans started moving out of the South to northern cities and western states. They wanted more choices, better jobs, and better schools. They wanted the same freedoms that other Americans had. African

Many African-Americans hoped that by moving elsewhere they could start a new—and better—life.

American neighborhoods grew, and people voted for local officials who would fight segregation. Many African Americans were killed for standing up for their rights.

In New York in the 1920s, African American business-people used their money to support African American artists, writers, and musicians. The "New Negro" would show his or her independence through talent and creativity. In the New York City neighborhood of Harlem, African Americans associated with the arts created their own unique culture and identity. This cultural movement became known as the Harlem Renaissance.

In New York, Harlem attracted tens of thousands of African Americans with the promise of new opportunity and the chance to celebrate their heritage.

There were still limitations on freedom for many African Americans. In many states, African Americans could not buy houses in "restricted" neighborhoods. They could ride only in seats at the back of buses. Many colleges were segregated, so African Americans had few opportunities to attend them. Regardless of their abilities, the attitudes of the white majority limited African Americans' opportunities.

One group of **activists** decided to form a group to fight for equality. In 1911, this group became the National Association for the Advancement of Colored People, or the NAACP. It worked to end segregation in housing, transportation, and education.

13

Jackie Robinson (far right) broke the "color line" in baseball, which was an important step toward bringing blacks and whites closer together.

STEPS TOWARD INTEGRATION

African American soldiers returned from fighting in Europe in World War II and hoped to find the nation more accepting of equality. After all, they had fought for their country as had white soldiers. Unfortunately, African Americans were still considered second-class citizens in 1945. Some change came about after President Harry Truman ended segregation in the U.S. military in 1948. Major-league baseball was integrated when Jackie Robinson was signed to play for the Brooklyn Dodgers. With renewed hope, the NAACP continued its fight to end segregation.

The Legal Defense Fund (LDF) was set up in 1939 as a branch of the NAACP. Lawyers at LDF worked to end inequality through legal means. At first, LDF took cases dealing with segregation in transportation and housing. Later, it would take cases dealing with segregation in education. The first cases it selected were those of students who had not been admitted to colleges and universities simply because they were African American. LDF attorneys knew that judges would see the inequality of having segregated law schools and would rule against segregation.

Officials of the NAACP worked together to decide which cases would have the greatest impact on their mission to fight inequality.

TAKING A CASE TO THE SUPREME COURT

The highest court in the United States is the U.S. Supreme Court. There are nine justices (judges) on the Supreme Court, and their job is to interpret, or explain, the laws. If the Supreme Court decides that a state has passed a law that violates the U.S. Constitution, then that law is declared unconstitutional.

Our country's most important legal issues are debated in the Supreme Court building shown above.

When a lawsuit was filed against a segregated school, the case would go either to a state court or to a federal district court. Once that lower court made a ruling, lawyers could **appeal** the ruling and ask that the case be heard by a higher court. Mostly, LDF lawyers tried cases that they could appeal to the U.S. Supreme Court.

The inequality between schools was easy to see. Schools for white children had clean, new facilities, and white teachers received higher pay than did African American teachers. White students traveled to school on school buses and learned from new textbooks. Schools for African American students were housed in older buildings that were overcrowded. Often, they had no auditoriums or gymnasiums; some had no indoor toilets. African Americans often walked miles to school because there were fewer African American schools and they were farther apart. There was usually no school bus to transport African American students.

A group of African-American children walks to school.

Courts often ruled in favor of African American plaintiffs when schools were unequal. (The person or people who have been harmed and are filing the suit are called the plaintiffs. The person or people against whom the suit is filed are called the defendants.) Judges ordered school districts to

Demonstrators marched in front of a school board office to protest school segregation.

provide equal facilities to both groups of students. Sometimes schools were made to look equal, but segregation continued.

THEIR DAY IN COURT

In 1950, seventeen states and the District of Columbia still had laws that required the existence of segregated schools. Four states had laws that permitted the existence of segregated schools. Only sixteen states had laws that **prohibited** the existence of segregated schools. Were these state laws unconstitutional? The NAACP wanted the U.S. Supreme Court to decide.

Thurgood Marshall, leader of the LDF attorneys, knew the U.S. Constitution very well. When he had gotten into trouble as a boy, the principal of Marshall's school made him read the Constitution until he had it memorized. Marshall knew that segregated schools were unconstitutional, but he and the LDF would have to prove it to the Supreme Court justices.

Thurgood Marshall's role in *Brown v. Board of Education* would make him one of the most well-known figures in the history of civil rights in America.

Marshall and others worked with local NAACP chapters to find just the right segregation cases to bring to the Court. The cases would need to have several plaintiffs so that if one decided to drop out, the case would not end. The lawyers would need to show clearly how these segregated schools were harmful to children. There could be no question in the justices' minds that segregation was illegal.

Autherine Lucy (shown right center) brought a case against the University of Alabama with the help of Thurgood Marshall and the NAACP. Hers was one of many cases related to inequality in schools.

By 1952, the NAACP had three cases of school segregation being heard by the U.S. Supreme Court. At the end of the session, however, the justices could not reach a decision. They scheduled to hear the cases a second time in their 1953 session. By 1953, two more cases had been added. The five combined cases were known as *Brown v. Board of Education*, the name of the case that originated in Topeka, Kansas.

FIVE CASES COME TOGETHER

The five cases that came before the U.S. Supreme Court represented students and parents in four states and the District of Columbia. The Court would decide if the four states of Kansas, Virginia, Delaware, and South Carolina had passed laws that violated citizens' rights under the Fourteenth Amendment. Because the District of Columbia is not governed by state law,

WHY TWICE?

The U.S. Supreme Court heard the combined cases of *Brown v. Board of Education* two times. In December 1952, when the case first came before the Court, the justices had several questions and needed more information. By 1953, Chief Justice Fred Vinson had died and was replaced by Earl Warren. This was enough to change the outcome of the *Brown* case. Justice Warren wanted—and worked to get—a **unanimous** decision from the Court against racial segregation in schools.

This photograph shows the Supreme Court justices in 1953, the year before they would make the landmark decision in *Brown v. Board of Education*.

21

***

the Court would decide if segregated schools violated students' rights to due process (not taking away property or opportunity without cause) under the Fifth Amendment.

BULAH V. GEBHART AND BELTON V. GEBHART

Shirley Bulah attended Hockessin Elementary School in a suburb of Wilmington, Delaware. A school bus for white children drove past her home every morning, but Shirley was not allowed to ride it. She had to walk 2 miles (3.2 kilometers) to her segregated school. Shirley's mother, Sarah, asked the Delaware Department of Public Instruction to allow Shirley to take the bus, but the department refused. Sarah Bulah filed suit against school officials.

NAMING A LAWSUIT

Legal cases get their names from the plaintiff and the defendant. Sometimes the plaintiff's and defendant's names are shortened and the Latin term *et al.* is added to mean "and all the others." When several cases are grouped together to be heard as one, they take the name of only one of the cases. *Brown et al. v. Board of Education of Topeka et al.* is named for the Topeka case. Oliver Brown was the first name on the list of plaintiffs in the Topeka case.

Supreme Court of the United States

No. 1 ——— , *October Term, 19* 54

Oliver Brown, Mrs. Richard Lawton, Mrs. Sadie Emmanuel et al.,

Appellants,

vs.

Board of Education of Topeka, Shawnee County, Kansas, et al.

This case was named after Oliver Brown, the first plaintiff listed in the Topeka case.

In the nearby community of Claymont, Ethel Louise Belton and her friends attended segregated Howard High School in downtown Wilmington, 20 miles (32 km) away. Howard High had three times as many students as did the white school in Claymont, but Howard High did not have as many classes and had almost no extracurricular, or after-school, activities. Ethel Belton and seven other parents asked the school board to make improvements at their children's school, but school board officials refused. Belton and the other parents filed suit against the school officials.

In 1929, attorney Louis Redding asked the NAACP to help in their case. The Delaware Court of Chancery ruled that the existence of segregated schools was unconstitutional and ordered that the children be admitted to the schools for white children immediately. The school board appealed the ruling, and the case went before the U.S. Supreme Court.

This run-down auditorium was part of Moton High School in Farmville. In an effort to improve the conditions in their school, students went on strike for two weeks.

DAVIS V. PRINCE EDWARD COUNTY

Robert Moton High School in Farmville, Virginia, was built to hold 180 students. By 1950, 450 African American students were crowded into the school. Some classes were even held on a school bus. In protest, students went on strike for two weeks. One hundred and seventeen students asked the school board to end segregation. When the board refused, the NAACP helped the students file suit. The case was named for Dorothy E. Davis, a fourteen-year-old student. Barbara Johns and Carrie Stokes were also listed as plaintiffs.

Experts on both sides were called to present their opinions during the trial. The school district experts argued that mixing African American students with white students would be dangerous, because violence between the students would break out. A psychologist for the NAACP testified that being segregated caused African American children to believe they were not as good or as smart as white children were.

The judges decided that having segregated schools in Virginia was legal and would continue. However, the students at Robert Moton High School had made a difference. Their protest inspired people across the nation to join the fight for equality and **desegregation**.

Across the nation, civil rights rallies began taking place. Here, thousands of Americans marched near the Lincoln Memorial in Washington, D.C.

* * * *

BRIGGS V. ELLIOTT

In 1950, nearly 70 percent of the population of Clarendon County, South Carolina, was African American. School principal Reverend J.A. DeLaine and Levi Pearson, a parent whose children attended the African American school in Clarendon County, asked the school board to provide buses for transporting African American students. The school board refused, saying that tax money was used to pay for the buses. African Americans did not pay much in taxes because they owned very little land and did not earn much money. White families would not think it fair to use

This photograph shows children in a black neighborhood in Columbia, South Carolina.

Harry Briggs, shown here in front of the Scott's Branch School in Summerton, South Carolina, filed a school desegregation lawsuit in 1950. Briggs would later lose his job as a result of his involvement in the case.

taxpayers' money to pay for buses for African American students. Levi Pearson filed suit to get transportation for his children, but his case was thrown out of court. Pearson's farm was on the county line; he paid taxes in District 5, but his children attended the segregated school intended for children living in Districts 22 and 26.

Rev. DeLaine continued the fight to provide transportation for African American students. He contacted the lawyers at the NAACP for help. Because of his fight, Rev. DeLaine was fired from his job as principal. However, he helped fourteen fathers and six mothers to challenge South Carolina's laws allowing segregated schools. The first name on the list was that of Harry Briggs, a service station attendant in Summerton and father of Harry Briggs, Jr.

IN THE DISTRICT COURT OF THE UNITED STATES
FOR THE EASTERN DISTRICT OF SOUTH CAROLINA
CHARLESTON DIVISION

FILED
JUN 23 1951
ERNEST L. ALLEN
C.R.C.U.S.E.D.S.C.

VOL 68 PAGE 59

HARRY BRIGGS, JR., et al,   Civil Action No. 2657

          Plaintiffs,

    vs.   DISSENTING OPINION

R. W. ELLIOTT, Chairman, et al,

          Defendants.

          This case has been brought for the express and declare
purpose of determining the right of the State of South Carolina,
in its public schools, to practice segregation according to race

          The Plaintiffs are all residents of Clarendon County,
South Carolina which is situated within the Eastern District of
South Carolina and within the jurisdiction of this court. The
Plaintiffs consist of minors and adults there being forty-six
minors who are qualified to attend and are attending the public
schools in School District 22 of Clarendon County; and twenty
adults who are taxpayers and are either guardians or parents of
the minor Plaintiffs. The Defendants are members of the Board
of Trustees of School District 22 and other officials of the
educational system of Clarendon County including the superin-
tendent of education. They are the parties in charge of the
various schools which are situated within the aforesaid school
district and which are affected by the matters set forth in this
cause.

          The Plaintiffs allege that they are discriminated
against by the Defendants under color of the Constitution and
laws of the State of South Carolina whereby they are denied
equal educational facilities and opportunities and that this
denial is based upon difference in race. And they show that the
school system of this particular school district and county
(following the general pattern that it is admitted obtains in

                              -1-

This document contains the opinion of Judge Waring in *Briggs vs. Elliott*. Judge Waring was the only member of the court who was against school segregation.

Three judges heard the Briggs case. The NAACP called Kenneth Clark, a **social scientist**, to testify. Clark had conducted studies with the children in Summerton's schools. Using two dolls—one black and one white—Clark asked the students to pick the nicest doll. He then asked the students to pick the doll most like them. He also asked the students to pick the doll they liked the best. African American students most often picked the white doll as the nicest and best, but picked the black doll as the one most like them.

Because of his studies, Dr. Clark believed that African American children suffered when they were forced to attend segregated schools. The children believed they were less important than white people and had low self-esteem. The court ruled that segregation in schools could continue, but the schools would have to be made equal so no more damage would be done to the students.

BROWN V. BOARD OF EDUCATION OF TOPEKA

Kansas law did not require any schools to be segregated. Instead, Kansas law allowed elementary schools in "cities of the first class" (those with more than 15,000 people) to segregate if the community agreed. Schools could only segregate

DR. CLARK: THE "DOLL DOCTOR"

Kenneth B. Clark (left) and his wife, Mamie, were social scientists. They studied the way African American children reacted to their environment. They used black and white dolls to test the children's ideas about race. When the NAACP asked Dr. Clark to testify, he was not sure his studies would be helpful. Clark became known as the "doll doctor" and was one of the first social scientists to testify in segregation cases.

in elementary grades (through the eighth grade), and schools for African American students had to be equal to schools for white students. In 1950, Topeka, Kansas, had eighteen schools for white students and four schools for African-American elementary students. All students attended the integrated high school.

When Topeka first established segregated schools, there were no junior high schools. Over time, junior high schools were set up for white students only. In 1941, a family in Topeka filed a lawsuit because no junior high schools had been set up for African American students. This meant that African Americans went to segregated schools through the eighth grade and then attended an integrated junior high for only one year. The Kansas Supreme Court decided that junior high schools were not to be segregated.

Here, an African American teacher is shown reading to his pupils at a segregated school in Virginia in 1947.

As students in the seventh and eighth grades from the segregated schools were moved into the integrated junior high schools, several African American teachers were fired because they were not allowed to teach in integrated schools. Because of this, many families in Topeka were afraid to question the legality of segregation in schools. They believed more African American teachers would be fired if schools integrated.

On the surface, Topeka schools seemed to be equal. Schools for African Americans and whites both were housed in well-kept buildings. Textbooks were nearly the same, although some of those used in the African American schools were a bit older. Teachers in the schools for African Americans were paid nearly the same as teachers in the schools for whites. African American children even rode buses to their schools because they were a distance away from their homes. There were no buses for the white children because their schools were in their own neighborhoods. Still, segregated schools were not equal. Lucinda Todd's daughter Nancy wanted to play the violin, but music classes were not offered to students at the African American schools.

McKinley Burnett was president of the Topeka NAACP. Burnett spent two years attending school board meetings to ask the Topeka Board of Education to integrate schools.

The NAACP attorneys were called in for help on the Topeka case.

When the school board ignored his request, Burnett contacted the NAACP for help.

The Topeka parents planned to show that the Kansas law allowing segregated schools to exist in some communities was harmful, even when the schools appeared to be equal. Thirteen parents signed as plaintiffs representing their twenty children against the Topeka Board of Education. Most of the parents were mothers, but one father volunteered to be a plaintiff. Oliver L. Brown represented his daughter, Linda.

Plaintiffs were carefully selected to show that they had to travel a great distance past a school for white students to attend the segregated school. The attorneys instructed the parents to take their children to their neighborhood school to enroll. After they were turned down and sent to the segregated school, the parents could show they had been harmed by not being able to enroll their students in their neighborhood school. The parents could then sign as plaintiffs.

The district court ruled that Topeka schools did not violate the state segregation law. As a result, the LDF attorneys added the Kansas case to those going before the U.S. Supreme Court. In this case, Topeka's schools appeared to be equal, so the issue was not about equality. Instead, the Court would have to determine if segregation itself violated the Fourteenth Amendment.

Thurgood Marshall talks with Spottswood Robinson III, a valued advisor to Marshall. They worked together on the Brown case.

BOLLING V. SHARPE

Judine Bishop attended Browne Junior High in Washington, D.C. Her father, Gardner Bishop, worked with other parents to bring public attention to segregation in the capital city. (As our nation's capital, Washington, D.C. is not governed by any state. Instead, the United States Congress makes laws to govern schools in the District of Columbia.) White students had plenty of space in their classrooms, but African American students were crowded into run-down buildings with small playgrounds. African American students used hand-me-down text-books that had been thrown away by the schools for white students. Even public playgrounds in the district were segregated.

A group of African American students pose on the steps outside Randall Jr. High in Washington, D.C.

Gardner Bishop and the Consolidated Parents Group organized a strike, hoping to force the school board to make changes. They contacted attorney Charles Hamilton Houston for help. Houston was an African American whose father had also been an attorney. He knew that people would be slow to change their attitudes, and that only the courts could bring real change. Before Houston could file the suit for the Consolidated Parents Group, however, he suffered a heart attack. James Nabrit, Jr. took over Houston's work.

Charles Hamilton Houston devoted much of his life to civil rights. He was the first African American lawyer to win a case before the Supreme Court.

Nabrit refused to file a suit just to demand equal schools. He told Bishop and the other parents that he would work only toward desegregation. To test the school board's policy on segregation, Nabrit had the Consolidated Parents Group take eleven African American students to enroll in the new John Philip Sousa Junior High School. The school board, of course, refused to admit the students. One of those students was Spottswood Thomas Bolling, the student for whom the case is named.

TIME FOR CHANGE

The Supreme Court's decision in *Brown v. Board of Education* would change history. The decision was unanimous. On May 17, 1954, the U.S. Supreme Court ruled that "separate but equal is inherently unequal." No state had the right to pass a law that violated citizens' rights listed in the Fourteenth Amendment. Chief Justice Earl Warren read aloud

Shown left to right, attorneys George E. C. Hayes, Thurgood Marshall, and James Nabrit, Jr. posed in front of the Supreme Court building after winning the *Brown* case.

the decision, his first as a Supreme Court justice. Deseg-regation was to take place with "all deliberate speed." This formality ended the case and legal segregation, but the ruling was not generally accepted. Because no specific deadline was given, several cities and states took years to integrate schools.

Some states began desegregating schools right away. Some, however, would fight desegregation to the bitter end. Southern states fought the hardest. In March 1956, a group of senators and representatives from nine states signed a document known as the "Southern Manifesto."

Journalists read newly-printed copies of the *Memphis World*, which printed a story about the Court's decision to end segregation in public schools.

Students at Clinton High School in Tennessee protested integration.

This document told the Supreme Court that these states would not accept the ruling, and that they would fight to keep from desegregating. "If [integration is] done, this is certain to destroy the system of public education in some of the States. . . . We pledge ourselves to use all lawful means to bring about a reversal of this decision which is contrary to the Constitution and to prevent the use of force in its implementation." They would close public schools, if necessary, to keep African American children from mixing with white children.

Black and white fourth graders at St. Martin School in Washington, D.C. run for the playground. The nation's capital was one of few places to act on the Court's ruling relatively quickly.

WHAT WAS THE COST?

Many people devoted years of their lives to ending segregation, and some lost their lives in the process. In South Carolina, Harry Briggs and his wife lost their jobs. Rev. DeLaine's house was burned to the ground in a mysterious fire. Students in Prince Edward County, Virginia, where Barbara Johns and her friends had gone on strike, lost their chance for an education. School leaders closed public schools for five years rather than desegregate them. Some African American students went to live with relatives or friends in other counties so they could get an education. Many African American students never finished school.

In Topeka, Kansas, schools had begun desegregating even before *Brown v. Board of Education* went before the Supreme Court. In the process of closing African American schools, however, many teachers lost their jobs. Schools in other cities in Kansas did not integrate as quickly—some took as long as twenty-five years.

MILESTONE FOR CIVIL RIGHTS

The Supreme Court's ruling in *Brown v. Board of Education* marked the beginning of change, but that change took years to come about. In Arkansas, Little Rock's Central High School was desegregated in 1957. Nine African American students were selected to attend the previously whites-only high school. These brave students, known as the "Little Rock Nine," became a symbol of courage in the struggle to integrate southern schools.

The fight for equality and equal opportunity for African Americans has continued for decades. In December 1955, Rosa Parks made history when she refused to give up her seat on a bus to a white man. The Reverend Martin Luther King,

Elizabeth Eckford, one of the Little Rock Nine, entered Central High School to shouts of protest on September 6, 1957.

Martin Luther King, Jr. waved to a crowd of more than 200,000 people gathered on the Mall during the March on Washington in 1963.

The contributions of many individuals, such as Minnie Jean Brown (left), one of the Little Rock Nine, paved the way for civil rights in America. Their achievements helped make America a better place.

Jr., proclaimed his dream of equality for all people in 1963 from the steps of the Lincoln Memorial in Washington, D.C.

Today, people of all races, colors, religions, and national origins work, study, and live side by side. Many people living in the United States today have never known segregation. We still judge people as "us" or "them," but we do not have laws to separate us. Change came through the actions of hundreds of very brave people, some whose names are lost to history. Their courage and strength, and their willingness to take action despite the cost, has made the United States a better place in which to live.

Glossary

activists—people who fight for a cause or idea

appeal—to ask a higher court to review a decision made by a lower court on a legal case

civil rights—the rights of personal liberty, especially those guaranteed by the U.S. Constitution

desegregation—the removal of segregation to allow people of all races to have the same rights and to occupy the same space at the same time

enslaved—when someone has been held against his or her will as property without recognizing that person's human or civil rights

integrated—blended or united in that people of all races interact freely

prohibited—prevented

segregated—divided for members of different groups
or races

separate but equal—the idea that allowed segregation,
but only when equal facilities were provided to
all groups

social scientist—a scientist who studies human behavior

unanimous—in complete agreement

unconstitutional—against the constitution of a state
or nation

1868

The Fourteenth Amendment is ratified (approved) by the states and added to the U.S. Constitution to define individual citizens' rights.

1896

The Supreme Court rules in *Plessy v. Ferguson* that a Louisiana law requiring separate but equal accommodations for whites and African Americans on railroad cars is legal.

1911

The NAACP is established.

1934

Charles Hamilton Houston begins working for the NAACP.

1936

Thurgood Marshall begins working for the NAACP.

# of Education

The U.S. Supreme Court hears the cases a second time, with two new cases added.

Brown v. Board of Education decision is announced by the Supreme Court.

The Legal Defense Fund is established as a part of the NAACP.

Three combined cases come before the U.S. Supreme Court as *Brown v. Board of Education of Topeka*.

The Supreme Court announces that desegregation must proceed "with all deliberate speed" in all states.

The Southern Manifesto is issued by senators and representatives from Southern states.

The "Little Rock Nine" begin attending classes at Central High School in Little Rock, Arkansas.

To Find Out More

BOOKS

Haskins, Jim. *The Day Martin Luther King Jr. Was Shot: A Photo History of the Civil Rights Movement.* New York: Scholastic, 1992.

Kent, Deborah. *Thurgood Marshall and the Supreme Court.* Danbury, CT: Children's Press, 1997.

Santella, Andrew. *The NAACP: An Organization Working to End Discrimination.* Brookshire, TX: Child's World, 2003.

Williges, Mel. *Days of Courage: The Little Rock Story.* Austin, TX: Raintree Steck-Vaughn, 1996.

ONLINE SITES

Brown v. Board of Education National Historic Site
http://www.nps.gov/brvb/pphtml/facts.html
(click on the Junior Ranger Program document)

PBS—American Experience, U.S. History for Kids
http://www.pbs.org/wgbh/amex/kids/civilrights/

Index

Bold numbers indicate illustrations.

About the Author

Diane L. Good is an education specialist with the Kansas State Historical Society in Topeka, Kansas. She develops multicultural history curricula for schools and has worked with the Brown Foundation for Excellence and Equity in Education to create educational materials for the Brown v. Board of Education National Historic Site in Topeka. Representing the Kansas State Historical Society, she served as a founding member of the Brown v. Board 50th Anniversary Coalition in Kansas and developed teaching resources for Coalition sponsored activities and programs. As the historical consultant for Free State Productions, Inc., she has extensively researched some twenty legal challenges to segregation in Kansas that came before Brown was filed. Good has graduate degrees in anthropology and library science.